Sing, Spell Read & Write

TOTAL LANGUAGE ARTS
Reading · Writing · Spelling · Phonics · Speaking · Comprehension · Thinking

K-1

Start Your Engines

Letter Recognition · Manuscript Writing · Phonics
Audio Discrimination · Cutting · Pasting · Coloring

by Sue Dickson
Artwork by Norma Portadino

International Learning Systems of North America, Inc.
St. Petersburg, FL 33716

ISBN: 1-56704-028-4

Printed in the United States of America
1996 Edition • Copyright 1993 Sue Dickson

What You Say Guides The Way

To the teacher: As you form each letter on the chalkboard keep repeating:

(For **A**) "Put your pencil on the start dot. Go 'down the slide' as shown by arrow #1 to the 'floor line.' Now put your pencil on the start dot again, and go 'down the slide' as shown by arrow #2 to the 'floor line.' Now put your pencil on the middle broken line and give Mr. A a nice belt . . . and be sure to go the way the arrow points, from the first slide line we made to the second one. That's big letter **A**! (Say name of letter.) Ă, ă, apple!" (Say letter sound as in Phonics Song.)

(For **a**) "Now we are going to make a **little letter a**. Listen carefully and watch! Put your pencil on the start dot. First go up to touch the middle broken line, then curve around to touch the floor, then curve up, go all the way up to the start dot, and then come straight down to the floor with a stick. There, we have it, little a. Little letter **a**! A, a, apple!"

Color, Cut, and Paste
Pictures for A🍎a

To the Teacher: Have students remove this page from book.
Identify items in pictures (alligator, ax, hen, ambulance, banana, ox, chair, and astronaut).
Have the students cut along dotted lines and paste the pictures that start with the letter **A** sound on the next page.

Name

My Pictures for

A a

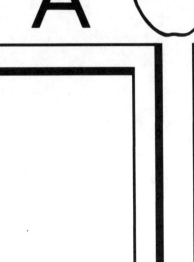

Directions: Have students remove page from book. Then have them paste the pictures that start with the correct letter sound into the frames.

My Magazine Picture for

A a

Directions: Have student cut a picture from a magazine and paste in the frame.

What You Say Guides The Way

To the teacher: As you form each letter on the chalkboard keep repeating:

(For **B**) "Put your pencil on the start dot. Go down straight to the floor. Now put your pencil on the start dot again; go around to the middle, then around to the floor! A big fat chest and a big fat tummy! That's big letter **B**! (Say name of letter.) Bh, bh, ball! (Say letter sound as in Phonics Song.)"

(For **b**) "Put your pencil on the start dot. Go straight down to the floor, bounce straight up to the middle dotted line, then around and down. **B**h! **B**h! Bounce up and around. **B**h! **B**h! Bounce up and around. (Repeat and repeat this.) Little letter **b**! Bh, bh, ball!"

B　B　B

b　b　b

Color, Cut, and Paste
Pictures for B b

To the Teacher: Have students remove this page from book.
Identify items in pictures (fish, balloon, elephant, key, beads, bird, baby, and clown).
Have the students cut along dotted lines and paste the pictures that start with the letter **B** sound on the next page.

Name _____

- -

My Pictures for

B  b

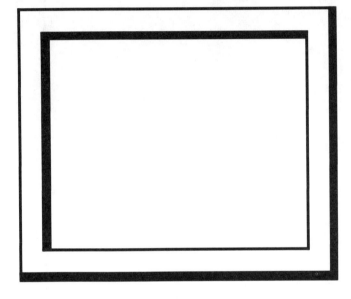 

Directions: Have students remove page from book. Then have them paste the pictures that start with the correct letter sound into the frames.

My Magazine Picture for

B b

Directions: Have student cut a picture from a magazine and paste in the frame.

It is an infringement of Copyright Law to reproduce these pages. Please **DO NOT COPY**

What You Say Guides The Way

To the teacher: As you form each letter on the chalkboard keep repeating:

(For **C**) "Put your pencil on the start dot. Go up to the ceiling, around to the floor and swing up. That's big letter **C**! (Say name of letter.) C, c, cat! (Say letter sound as in Phonics Song.)"

(For **c**) "Put your pencil on the start dot. Curve up to touch the middle broken line, then curve around and down to the floor line, then curve up just a bit. Little letter **c**! C, c, cat!"

C C C

C C C

Color, Cut, and Paste
Pictures for C  c

To the Teacher: Have students remove this page from book.
Identify items in pictures (corn, hand, cat, pan, flower, candle, cap, and net).
Have the students cut along dotted lines and paste the pictures that start with the letter **C** sound on the next page.

Name _____

_ _

My Pictures for
C  c

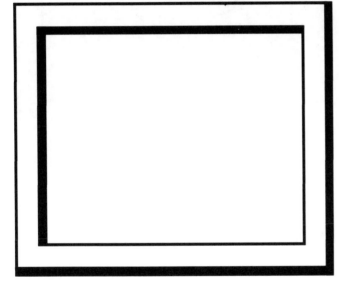

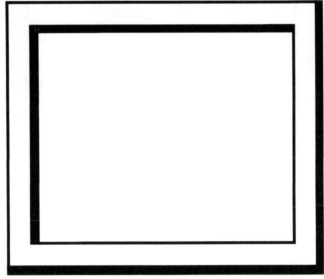

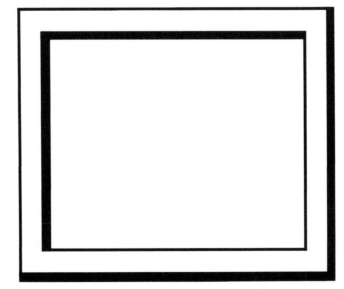

Directions: Have students remove page from book. Then have them paste the pictures that start with the correct letter sound into the frames.

My Magazine Picture for

C   c

Directions: Have student cut a picture from a magazine and paste in the frame.

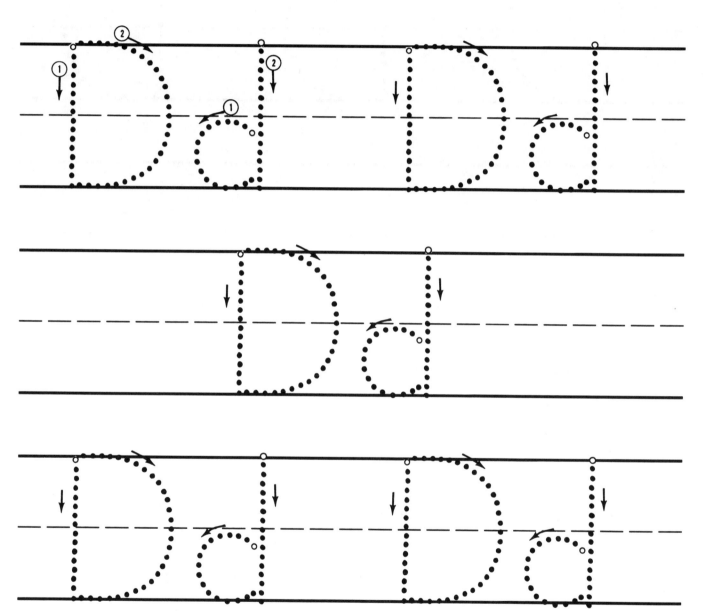

What You Say Guides The Way

To the teacher: As you form each letter on the chalkboard keep repeating:

(For **D**) "Put your pencil on the start dot. Go straight down to touch the floor. Put your pencil on the start dot again. Go around and down to the floor. That's big letter **D**! (Say name of letter.) D, d, doll! (Say letter sound as in Phonics Song.)"

(For **d**) "First make a little c from its start dot. Now put your pencil on the dot on the line above and come straight down to the floor, touching the edges of little c. First little c, then little d. (Repeat and repeat this.) Little letter **d**! D, d, doll!"

D D D

d d d

Color, Cut, and Paste
Pictures for D d

To the Teacher: Have students remove this page from book.
Identify items in pictures (doughnut, flag, envelope, duck, bed, doll, butterfly, and dog).
Have the students cut along dotted lines and paste the pictures that start with the letter **D** sound on the next page.

Name

My Pictures for

D d

Directions: Have students remove page from book. Then have them paste the pictures that start with the correct letter sound into the frames.

© 1993 Sue Dickson, International Learning Systems   It is an infringement of Copyright Law to reproduce these pages. Please **DO NOT COPY**

My Magazine Picture for

D d

Directions: Have student cut a picture from a magazine and paste in the frame.

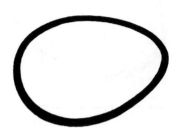

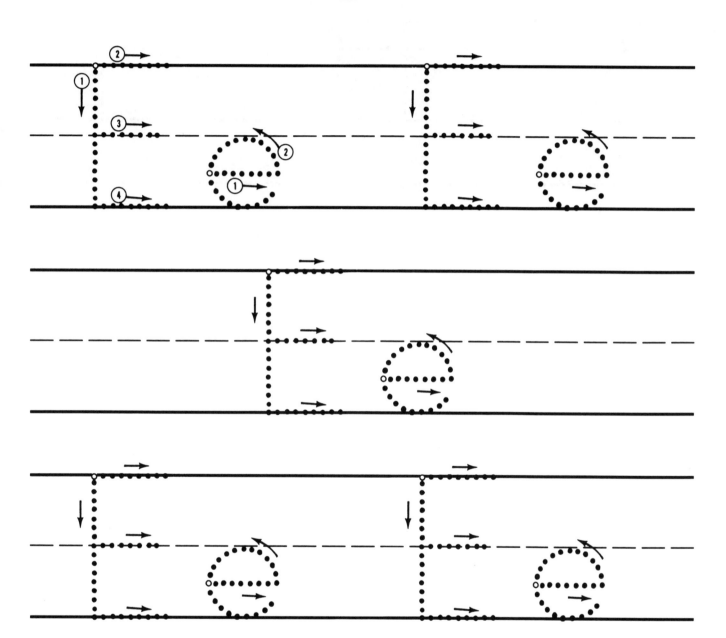

What You Say Guides The Way

To the teacher: As you form each letter on the chalkboard keep repeating:

(For **E**) "Put your pencil on the start dot. Go straight down to touch the floor, then across with his hat, across with his belt, and across with his shoes. That's Mr. **E**! (Say name of letter.) Ē, ĕ, egg! (Say letter sound as in Phonics Song.)"

(For **e**) "Put your pencil on the start dot which is **in the middle of the space** between the middle broken line and the floor, and make a line straight over the way we did for Mr. E's belt. Do not pick up your pencil, but curve up to the middle broken line and then make a 'c'. What do we have? Little letter **e**! E, e, egg!"

Color, Cut, and Paste
Pictures for **E** ⬭ **e**

To the Teacher: Have students remove this page from book.
Identify items in pictures (gum, jar, eggs, book, king, elbow, envelope, and an elephant).
Have the students cut along dotted lines and paste the pictures that start with the letter **E** sound on the next page.

Name _____

- -

My Pictures for

E ⬭ e

Directions: Have students remove page from book. Then have them paste the pictures that start with the correct letter sound into the frames.

My Magazine Picture for

E ⬭ e

Directions: Have student cut a picture from a magazine and paste in the frame.

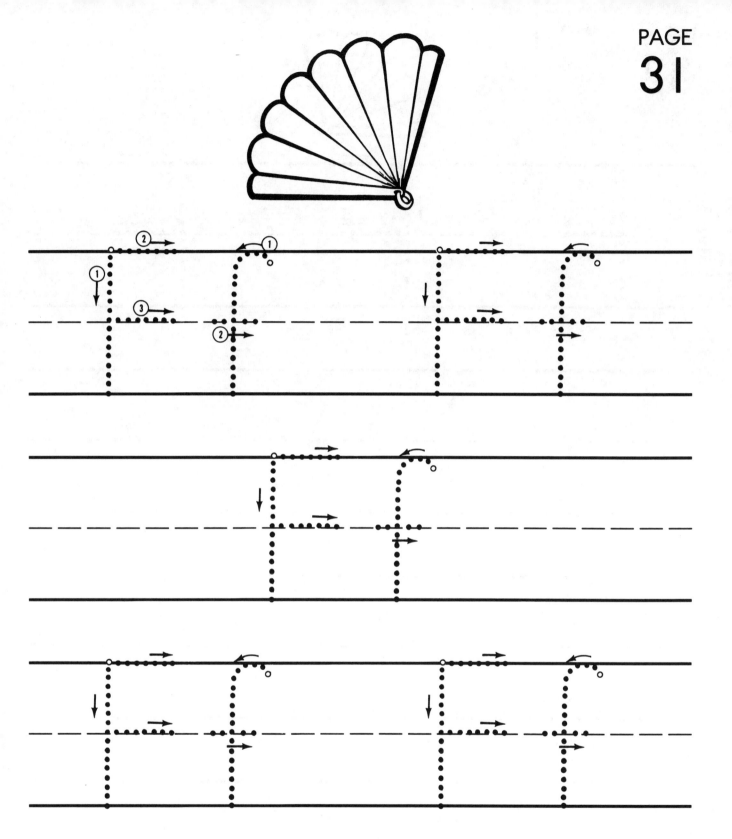

What You Say Guides The Way

To the teacher: As you form each letter on the chalkboard keep repeating:

(For **F**) "Put your pencil on the start dot. Go straight down to touch the floor, then across for a hat, across for a belt. That's big letter **F**! (Say name of letter.) F, f, fan! (Say letter sound as in Phonics Song.)"

(For **f**) "Put your pencil on the start dot. Up, the way we begin c, then straight to the floor, and a belt all the way across. Little letter **f**! F, f, fan!"

Color, Cut, and Paste
Pictures for F f

To the Teacher: Have students remove this page from book.
Identify items in pictures (hammer, fork, flag, shoe, turtle, fence, flowers, and a bell).
Have the students cut along dotted lines and paste the pictures that start with the letter **F** sound on the next page.

Name _____

My Pictures for

F   f

Directions: Have students remove page from book. Then have them paste the pictures that start with the correct letter sound into the frames.

© 1993 Sue Dickson, International Learning Systems   It is an infringement of Copyright Law to reproduce these pages. Please **DO NOT COPY**

My Magazine Picture for

F  f

Directions: Have student cut a picture from a magazine and paste in the frame.

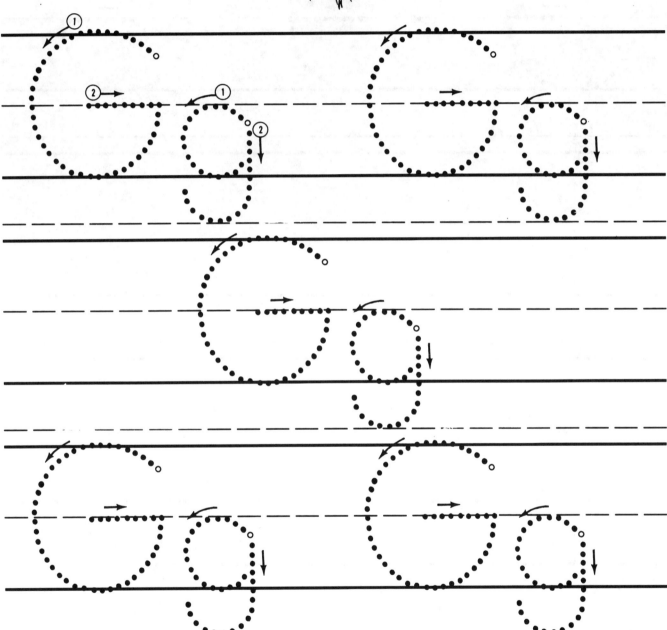

What You Say Guides The Way

To the teacher: As you form each letter on the chalkboard keep repeating:

(For **G**) "Put your pencil on the start dot. First make big C, and curve up to the middle broken line. Now give him a tray to hold! That's big letter **G**! (Say name of letter.) G, g, goat! (Say letter sound as in Phonics Song.)"

(For **g**) "Put your pencil on the start dot. First make little a, then go straight down through the floor to the next line and curve around to make a basket." "Say: "**G**ee, that's a good idea, a basket to catch the ball if it falls! **g**ee! Little letter **g**! G, g, goat!"

G   G   G

g   g   g

Color, Cut, and Paste
Pictures for G g

To the Teacher: Have students remove this page from book.
Identify items in pictures (gate, ruler, kite, goat, letter, needle, girl, and gum).
Have the students cut along dotted lines and paste the pictures that start with the letter **G** sound on the next page.

Name _____

- -

_____

My Pictures for

G  g

Directions: Have students remove page from book. Then have them paste the pictures that start with the correct letter sound into the frames.

My Magazine Picture for

G  g

Directions: Have student cut a picture from a magazine and paste in the frame.

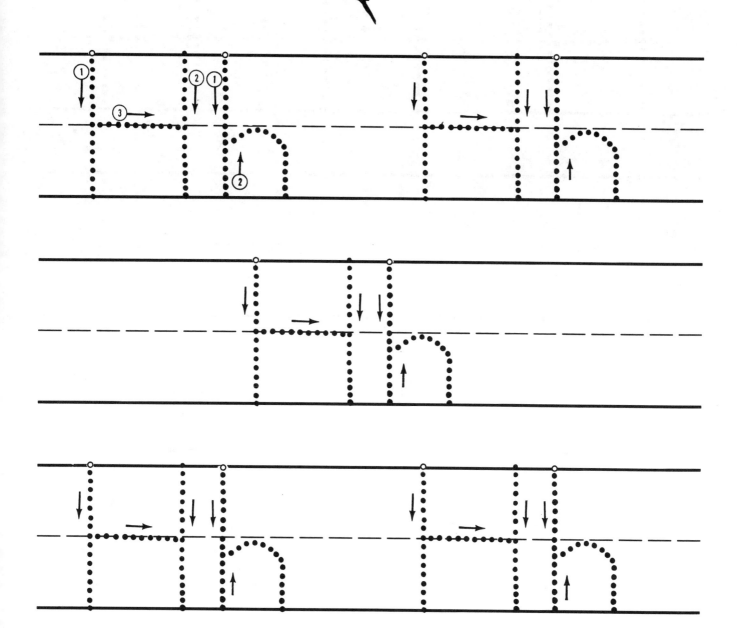

What You Say Guides The Way

To the teacher: As you form each letter on the chalkboard keep repeating:

(For **H**) "Put your pencil on the start dot and go straight down the floor. Now pick up your pencil and make another line just like that one just over a bit from the first one. Now make a bridge between the two. That's big letter **H**! (Say name of letter.) H, h, hand! (Say letter sound as in Phonics Song.)"

(For **h**) "Put your pencil on the start dot. Go down to the floor, up to the middle broken line, around and down. Little letter **h**! H, h, hand!"

Color, Cut, and Paste
Pictures for H h

To the Teacher: Have students remove this page from book.
Identify items in pictures (octopus, pig, hand, hat, moon, hose, heart, ball and bat).
Have the students cut along dotted lines and paste the pictures that start with the letter **H** sound on the next page.

Name

My Pictures for

H  h

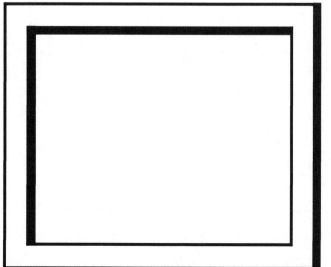
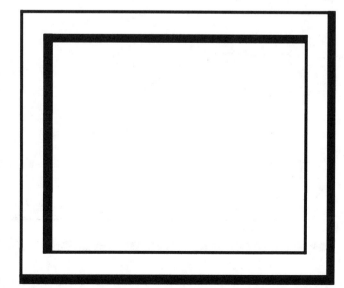

Directions: Have students remove page from book. Then have them paste the pictures that start with the correct letter sound into the frames.

My Magazine Picture for

H  h

Directions: Have student cut a picture from a magazine and paste in the frame.

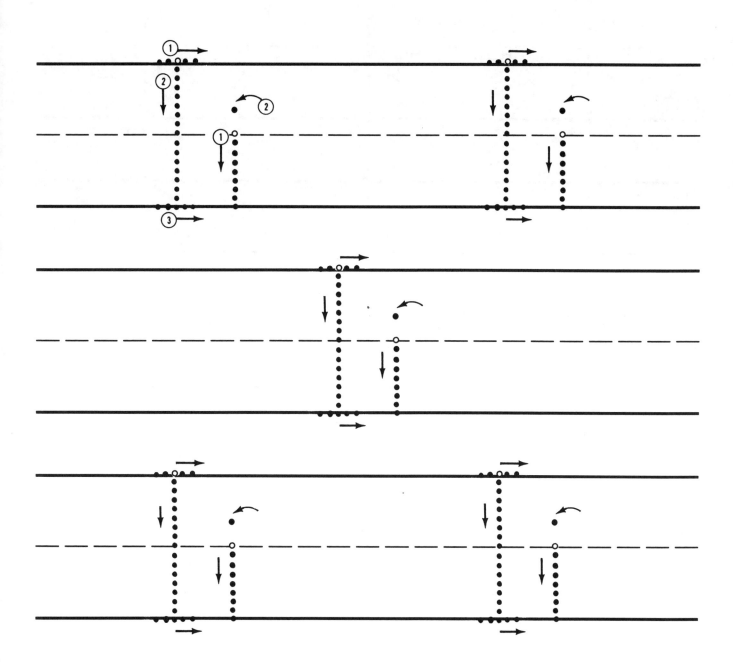

What You Say Guides The Way

To the teacher: As you form each letter on the chalkboard keep repeating:

(For **I**) "Put your pencil on the start dot and go straight down to the floor. Now give him a straight line for a headdress, and a straight line for moccasins. That's big letter **I**! (Say name of letter.) Ĭ, ĭ, Indian! (Say letter sound as in Phonics Song.)

(For **i**) "Put your pencil on the start dot and go down to the floor. Now give him a feather just above the middle line. Little letter **i**! I, i, Indian!"

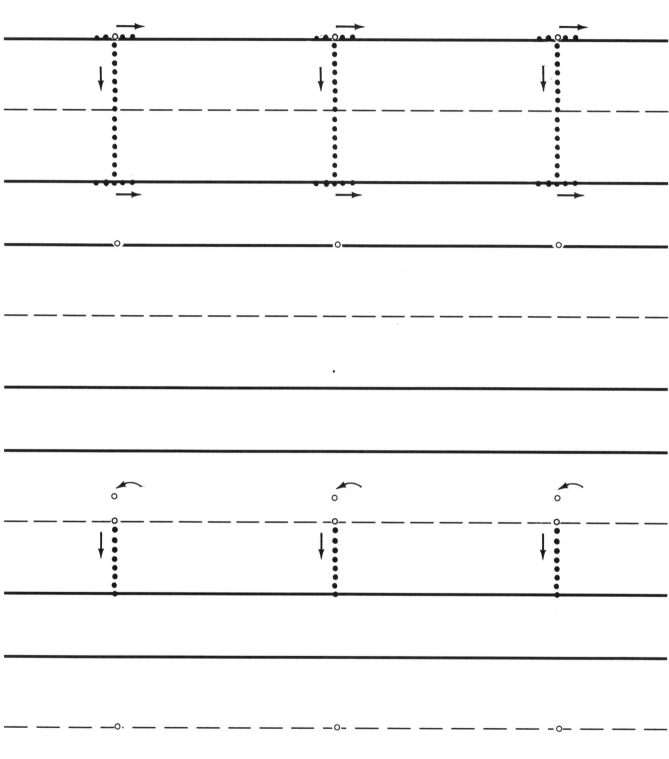

Color, Cut, and Paste
Pictures for I i

To the Teacher: Have students remove this page from book.
Identify items in pictures (igloo, telephone, stairs, Indian, itch, rain, ink, and peanuts).
Have the students cut along dotted lines and paste the pictures that start with the letter **I** sound on the next page.

Name

My Pictures for

I   i

Directions: Have students remove page from book. Then have them paste the pictures that start with the correct letter sound into the frames.

My Magazine Picture for

I  i

Directions: Have student cut a picture from a magazine and paste in the frame.

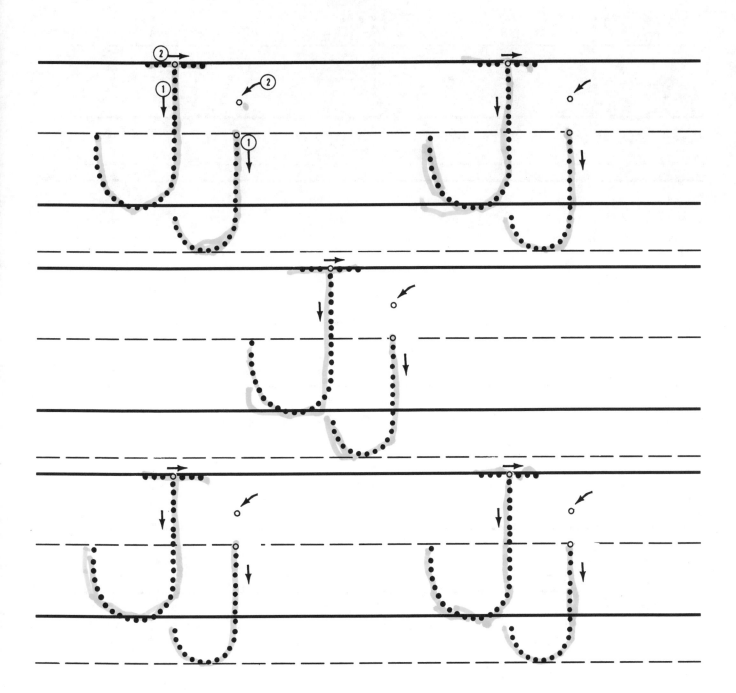

What You Say Guides The Way

To the teacher: As you form each letter on the chalkboard keep repeating:

(For **J**) "Put your pencil on the start dot and go straight down to the floor, then turn to make a basket just as you did for little g. Give it a straight line for a hat. That's big letter **J**! (Say name of letter.) J, j, jam! (Say letter sound as in Phonics Song.)"

(For **j**) "Put your pencil on the start dot and go down through the floor to the basement and make a basket, just as you did for big **J**. Now give it a dot. Little letter **j**! J, j, jam!"

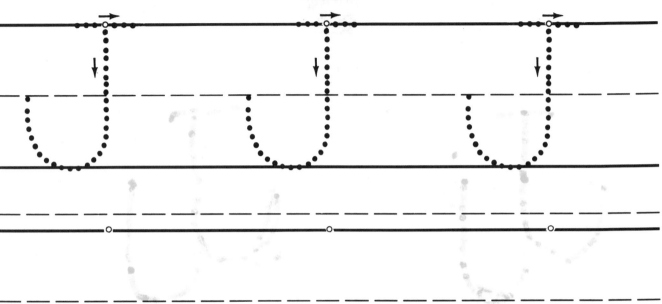

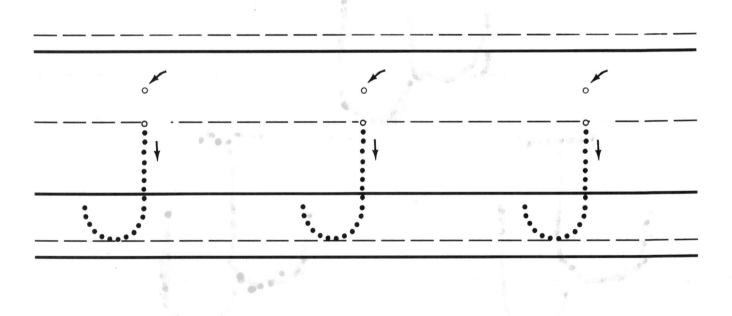

Color, Cut, and Paste
Pictures for J 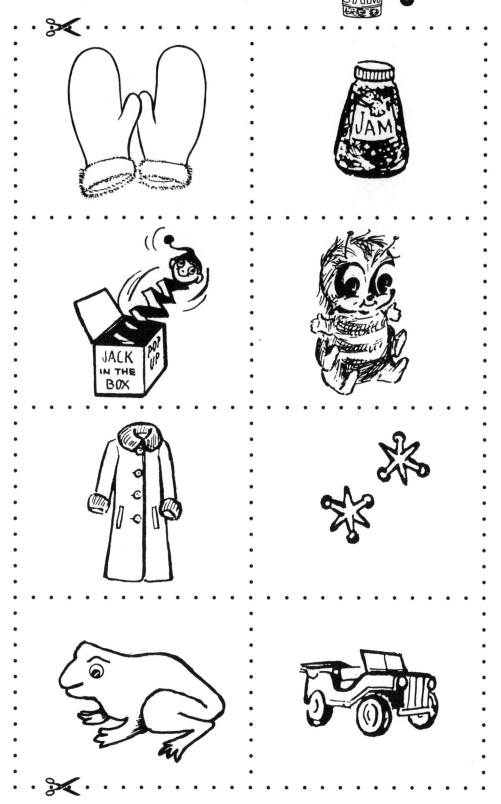 j

To the Teacher: Have students remove this page from book.
Identify items in pictures (mittens, jam, jack-in-the-box, bug, coat, jacks, frog, and a jeep).
Have the students cut along dotted lines and paste the pictures that start with the letter **J** sound on the next page.

Name

My Pictures for

J  j

Directions: Have students remove page from book. Then have them paste the pictures that start with the correct letter sound into the frames.

© 1993 Sue Dickson, International Learning Systems   It is an infringement of Copyright Law to reproduce these pages. Please **DO NOT COPY**

My Magazine Picture for

J J

j

Directions: Have student cut a picture from a magazine and paste in the frame.

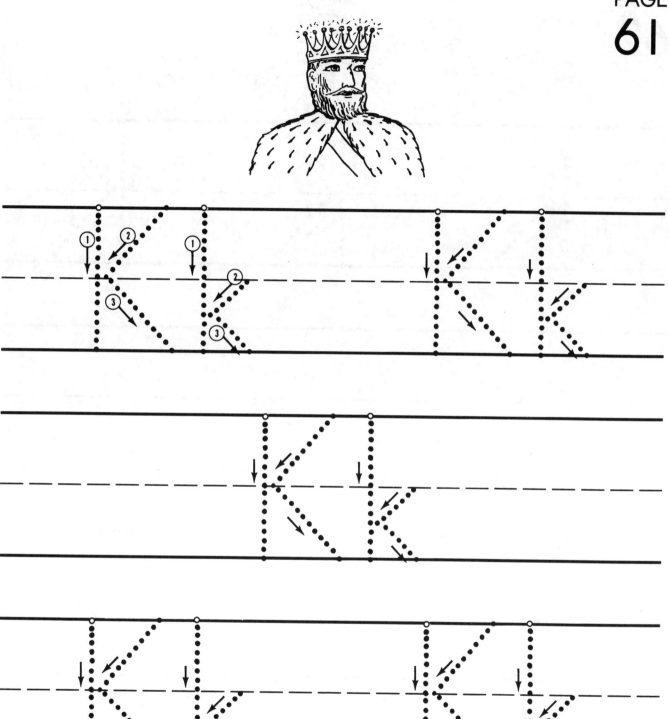

What You Say Guides The Way

To the teacher: As you form each letter on the chalkboard keep repeating:

(For **K**) "Put your pencil on the start dot and go straight down to the floor. Now put your pencil on the top line again and just a bit away from the start dot. Come down to the middle, then down to the floor. That's big letter **K**! (Say name of letter.) K, k, king! (Say letter sound as in Phonics Song.)

(For **k**) "Put your pencil on the start dot at the top line and go down to the floor. Put your pencil on the middle broken line and slant into the middle, as shown by arrow #2. Slant out and down to the base line, as arrow #3 indicates. That's little letter **k**! K, k, king!"

K K K

K K K

Color, Cut, and Paste
Pictures for K k

To the Teacher: Have students remove this page from book.
Identify items in pictures (pumpkin, kangaroo, kite, chicken, key, sailboat, king, and umbrella).
Have the students cut along dotted lines and paste the pictures that start with the letter **K** sound on the next page.

Name

My Pictures for

K   k

Directions: Have students remove page from book. Then have them paste the pictures that start with the correct letter sound into the frames.

© 1993 Sue Dickson, International Learning Systems   It is an infringement of Copyright Law to reproduce these pages. Please **DO NOT COPY**

My Magazine Picture for

K  k

Directions: Have student cut a picture from a magazine and paste in the frame.

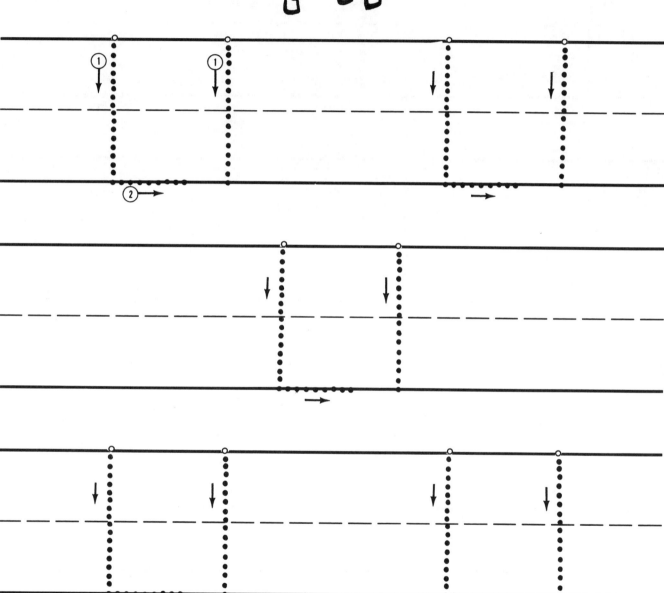

What You Say Guides The Way
To the teacher: As you form each letter on the chalkboard keep repeating:
(For **L**) "Put your pencil on the start dot. Go straight down, then turn the corner. That's big letter **L**! (Say name of letter.) L, l, lamb! (Say letter sound as in Phonics Song.)"
(For **l**) "Put your pencil on the start dot. Go straight down to the floor. Little letter **l**! L, l, lamb!"

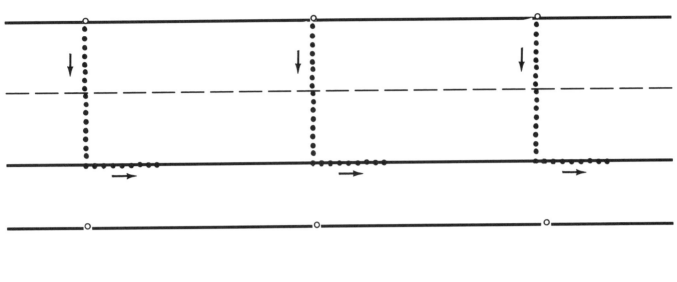

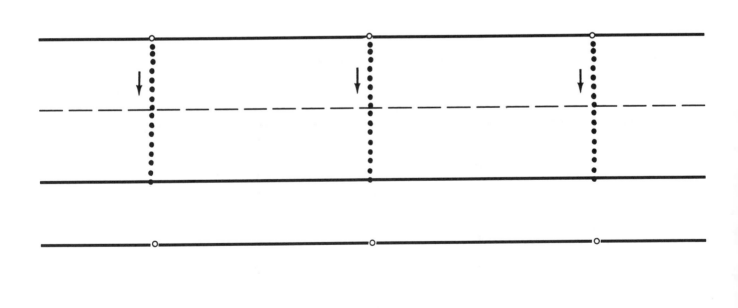

Color, Cut, and Paste
Pictures for L l

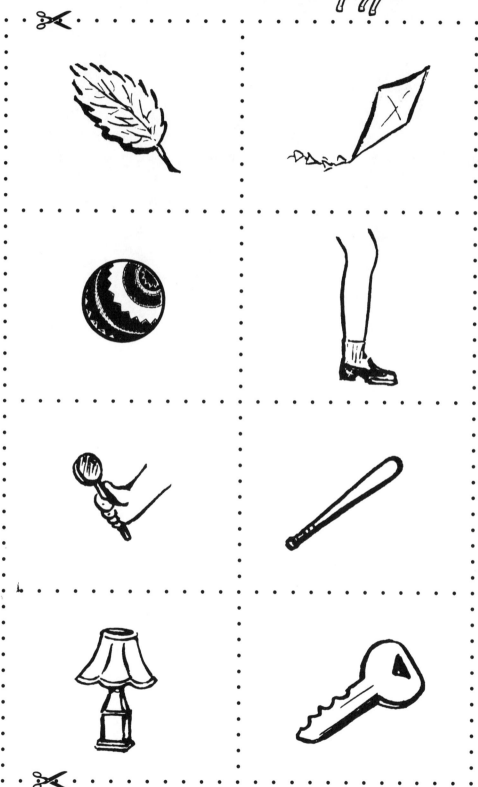

To the Teacher: Have students remove this page from book.
Identify items in pictures (leaf, kite, ball, leg, lollipop, bat, lamp, and key).
Have the students cut along dotted lines and paste the pictures that start with the letter **L** sound on the next page.

Name

My Pictures for

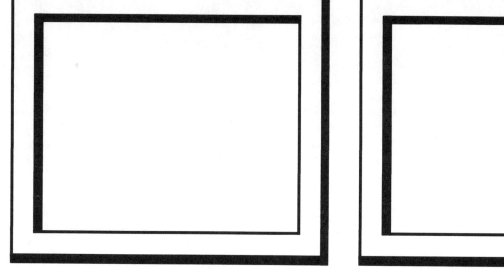 L l

My Magazine Picture for

L  l

Directions: Have student cut a picture from a magazine and paste in the frame.

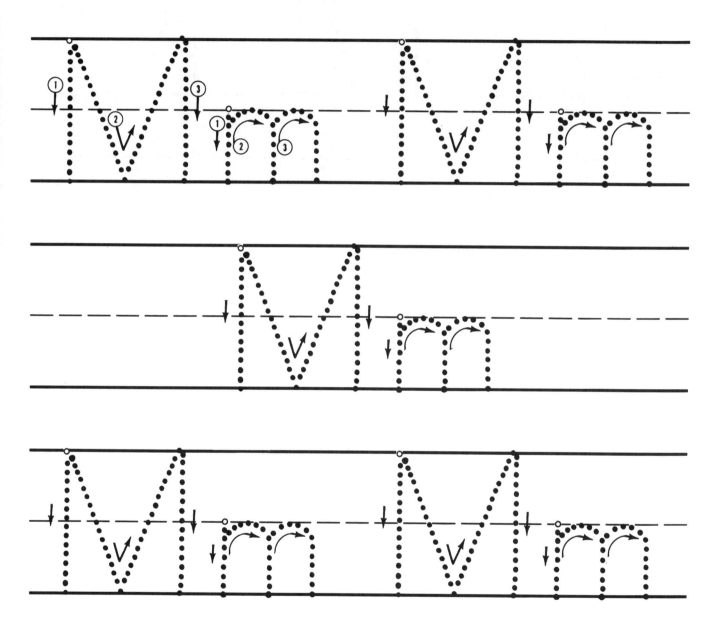

What You Say Guides The Way

To the teacher: As you form each letter on the chalkboard keep repeating:

(For **M**) "Put your pencil on the start dot. Go straight down to the floor. Put your pencil back on the start dot and go down the slide to the floor, up the slide to the top line, then straight down to the floor. Big letter **M**! (Say name of letter.) M, m, man! (Say letter sound as in Phonics Song.)"

(For **m**) "Put your pencil on the start dot. Go down to the floor, then go up on the same line almost to the top, then hump over and down, then up on the same line, then over and down again. Be sure to have each hump touch the middle broken line. Little letter **m**! M, m, man!"

Color, Cut, and Paste
Pictures for M ![image] m

To the Teacher: Have students remove this page from book.
Identify items in pictures (mouse, mitt, monkey, eggs, horn, leaf, glasses, and mop).
Have the students cut along dotted lines and paste the pictures that start with the letter **M** sound on the next page.

Name

My Pictures for

M  m

Directions: Have students remove page from book. Then have them paste the pictures that start with the correct letter sound into the frames.

My Magazine Picture for

M  m

Directions: Have student cut a picture from a magazine and paste in the frame.

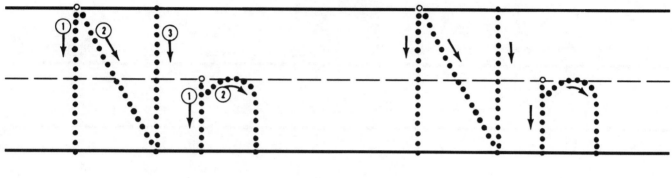

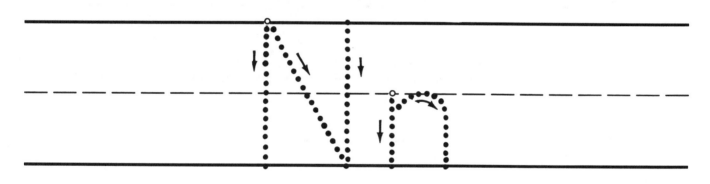

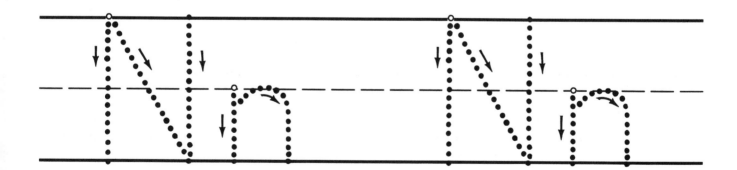

What You Say Guides The Way

To the teacher: As you form each letter on the chalkboard keep repeating:

(For **N**) "Put your pencil on the start dot. Go down to the floor. Put your pencil back on the start dot and go down the slide to the floor. Put your pencil on the top line again and go straight to the floor to touch the bottom of the slide. Big letter **N**! (Say letter sound as in Phonics Song.) N, n, nickel! (Say letter sound as in Phonics Song.)

(For **n**) "Put your pencil on the start dot. Go down to the floor, then go up on the same line almost to the top, then hump over and down to the floor again. Be sure to have hump touch the middle broken line. Little letter **n**! N, n, nickel!"

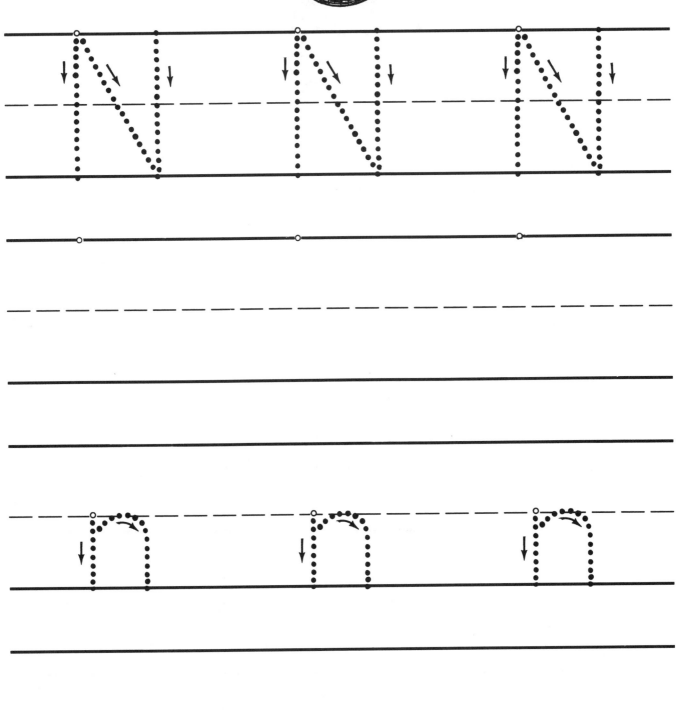

Color, Cut, and Paste Pictures for N n

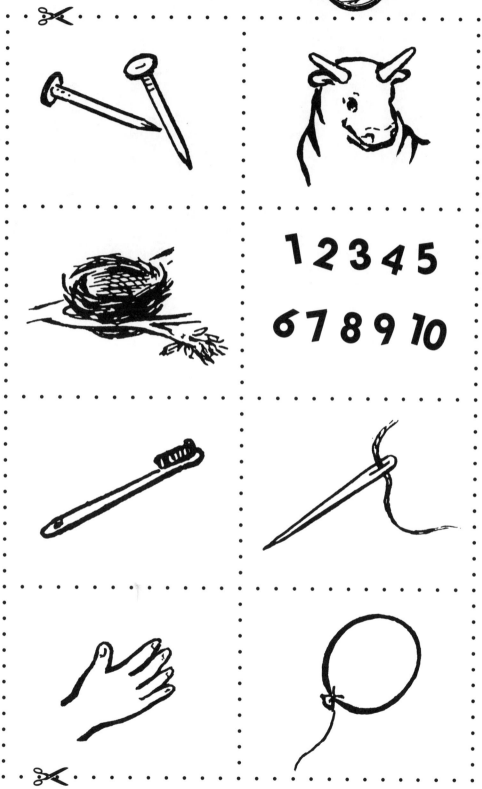

To the Teacher: Have students remove this page from book.
Identify items in pictures (nails, ox, nest, numbers, toothbrush, needle, hand, and balloon).
Have the students cut along dotted lines and paste the pictures that start with the letter **N** sound on the next page.

Name _____

- -

_____

My Pictures for

N n

Directions: Have students remove page from book. Then have them paste the pictures that start with the correct letter sound into the frames.

© 1993 Sue Dickson, International Learning Systems
It is an infringement of Copyright Law to reproduce these pages. Please **DO NOT COPY**

My Magazine Picture for

N n

Directions: Have student cut a picture from a magazine and paste in the frame.

It is an infringement of Copyright Law to reproduce these pages. Please **DO NOT COPY**

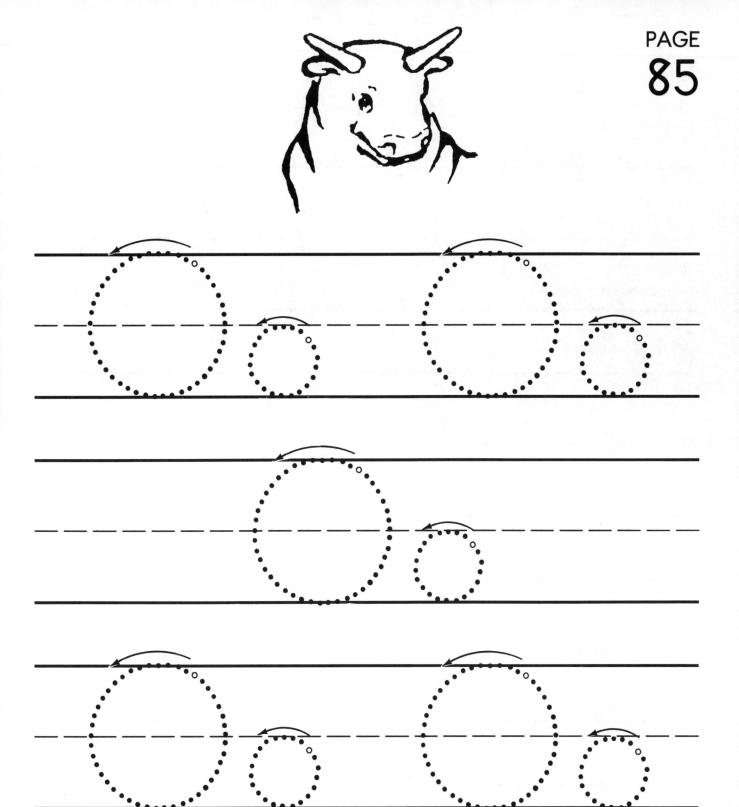

What You Say Guides The Way

To the teacher: As you form each letter on the chalkboard keep repeating:

(For **O**) "Put your pencil on the start dot. Curve up to touch the ceiling, then down to touch the floor, and up to where your started. Big letter **O**! (Say name of letter.) Ŏ, ŏ, ox! (Say letter sound as in Phonics Song.)"

(For **o**) "Put your pencil on the start dot. Curve up to touch the broken line, then down to touch the floor, and up to where you started. Little letter **o**! O, o, ox!"

Color, Cut, and Paste
Pictures for O 🐂 o

To the Teacher: Have students remove this page from book.
Identify items in pictures (wishbone, slippers, October, octopus, ox, chair, buttons and ostrich).
Have the students cut along dotted lines and paste the pictures that start with the letter **O** sound on the next page.

© 1993 Sue Dickson, International Learning Systems

Name

My Pictures for

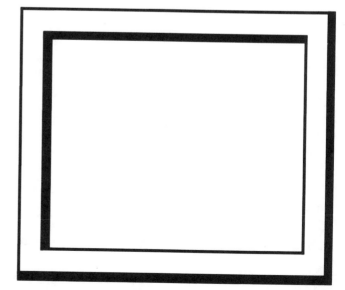

Directions: Have students remove page from book. Then have them paste the pictures that start with the correct letter sound into the frames.

It is an infringement of Copyright Law to reproduce these pages. Please **DO NOT COPY**

My Magazine Picture for

O o

Directions: Have student cut a picture from a magazine and paste in the frame.

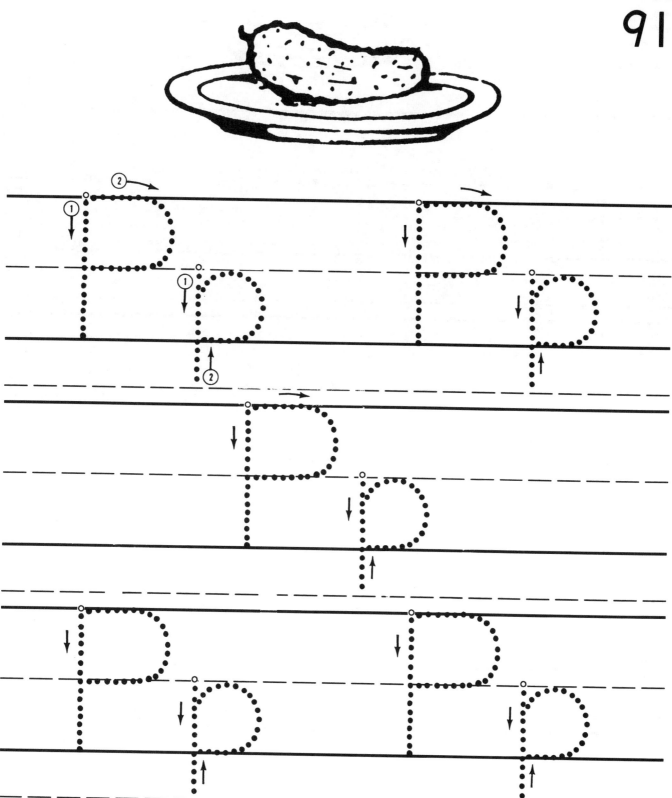

What You Say Guides The Way
To the teacher: As you form each letter on the chalkboard keep repeating:
(For **P**) "Put your pencil on the start dot and go straight down to the floor. Put your pencil on the start dot again and curve around to the center line. That's big letter **P**! (Say name of letter.) P, p, pickle! (Say letter sound as in Phonics Song.)"
(For **p**) "Put your pencil on the start dot and go down through the floor to the basement. Come right back up on that same line to the top and curve around to touch the floor line. That's little letter **p**! P, p, pickle!"

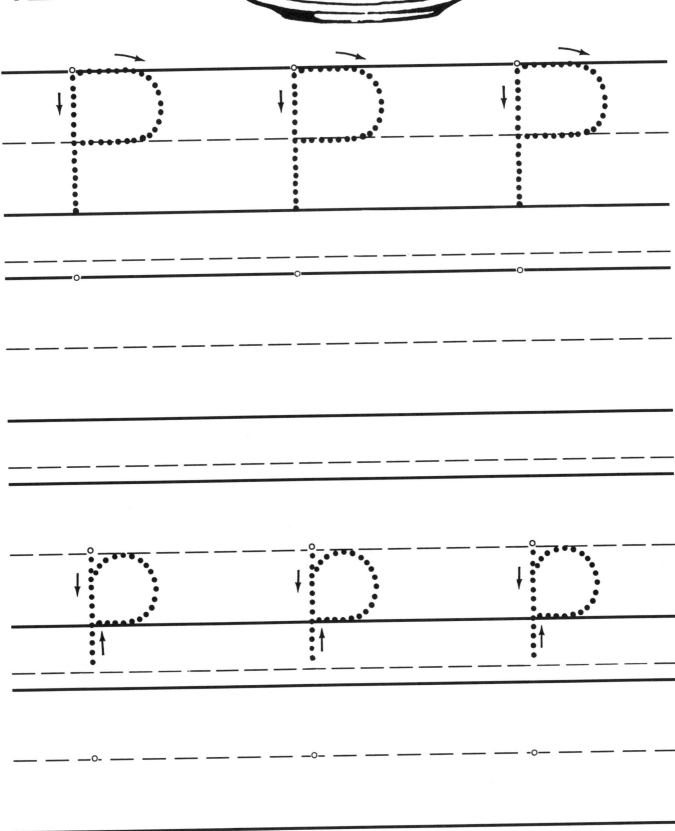

Color, Cut, and Paste
Pictures for Pp

To the Teacher: Have students remove this page from book.
Identify items in pictures (peanuts, lollipop, mittens, ring, shoe, pumpkin, puzzle, and a puppy).
Have the students cut along dotted lines and paste the pictures that start with the letter **P** sound on the next page.

Name _____

My Pictures for

P  p

Directions: Have students remove page from book. Then have them paste the pictures that start with the correct letter sound into the frames.

My Magazine Picture for

P  p

Directions: Have student cut a picture from a magazine and paste in the frame.

What You Say Guides The Way

To the teacher: As you form each letter on the chalkboard keep repeating:

(For **Q**) "Put your pencil on the start dot. Make capital O and then give the queen a walking stick. That's big letter **Q**! (Say name of letter.) Q, q, queen! (Say letter sound as in Phonics Song.)"

(For **q**) "Put your pencil on the start dot. Make little letter a, and go on straight down through the floor to the basement line and then curve to make a basket away from the ball. That's quizzical, if the ball falls it won't go into the basket. Q, q, quizzical! Q, q queen! That's little letter **q**!"

PAGE
98

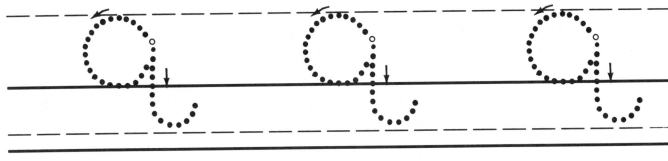

Color, Cut, and Paste
Pictures for Q q

PAGE
99

To the Teacher: Have students remove this page from book.
Identify items in pictures (quack, pipe, quarter, question mark, truck, quilt, hat, and a fork).
Have the students cut along dotted lines and paste the pictures that start with the letter **Q** sound on the next page.

Name

My Pictures for

Directions: Have students remove page from book. Then have them paste the pictures that start with the correct letter sound into the frames.

My Magazine Picture for

Q q

Directions: Have student cut a picture from a magazine and paste in the frame.

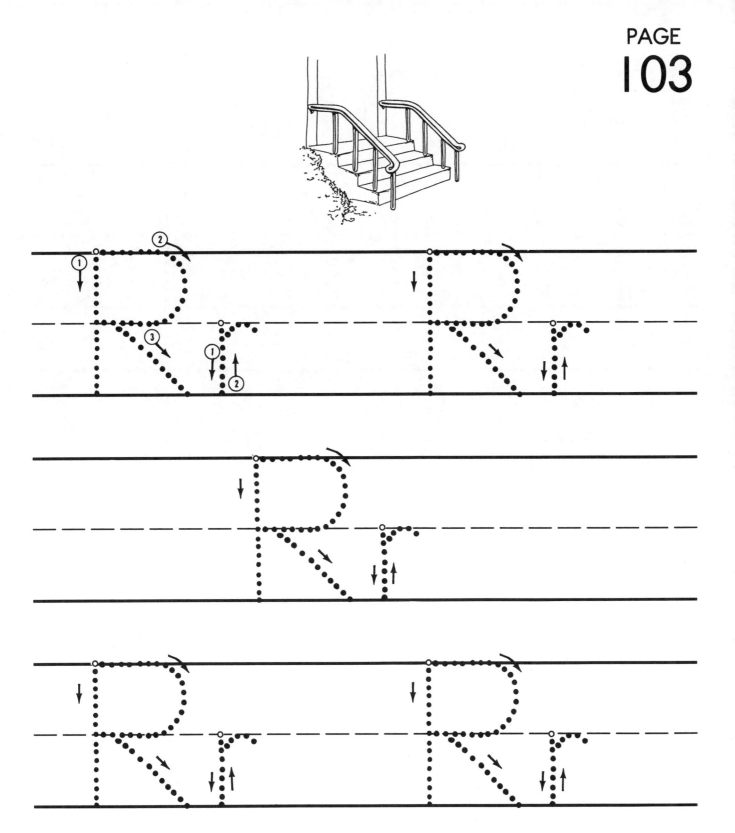

What You Say Guides The Way

To the teacher: As you form each letter on the chalkboard keep repeating:

(For **R**) "Put your pencil on the start dot. Form capital P and then give it a good leg down to the floor. That's big letter **R**! (Say name of letter.) R, r, rail! (Say letter sound as in Phonics Song.)"

(For **r**) "Put your pencil on the start dot. Go down, then up on the same line, and hook over. Little letter **r**! R, r, rail!"

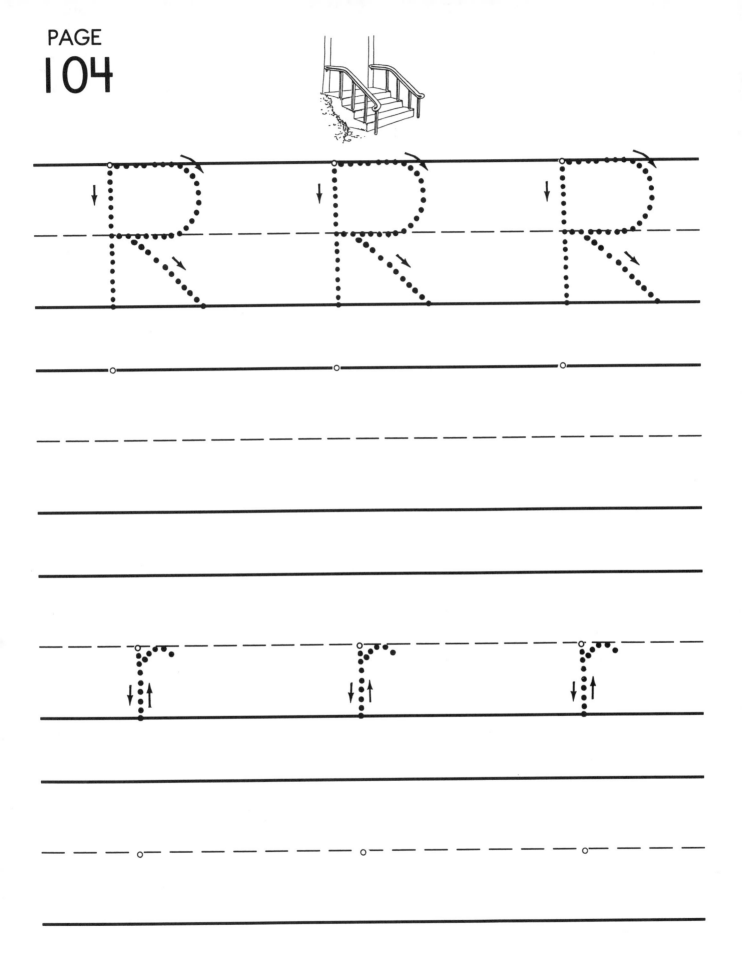

Color, Cut, and Paste
Pictures for R r

To the Teacher: Have students remove this page from book.
Identify items in pictures (hands, rake, present, rocket, rug, rattle, number 10, and mouse.
Have the students cut along dotted lines and paste the pictures that start with the letter **R** sound on the next page.

Name

My Pictures for

R r

Directions: Have students remove page from book. Then have them paste the pictures that start with the correct letter sound into the frames.

My Magazine Picture for

R  r

Directions: Have student cut a picture from a magazine and paste in the frame.

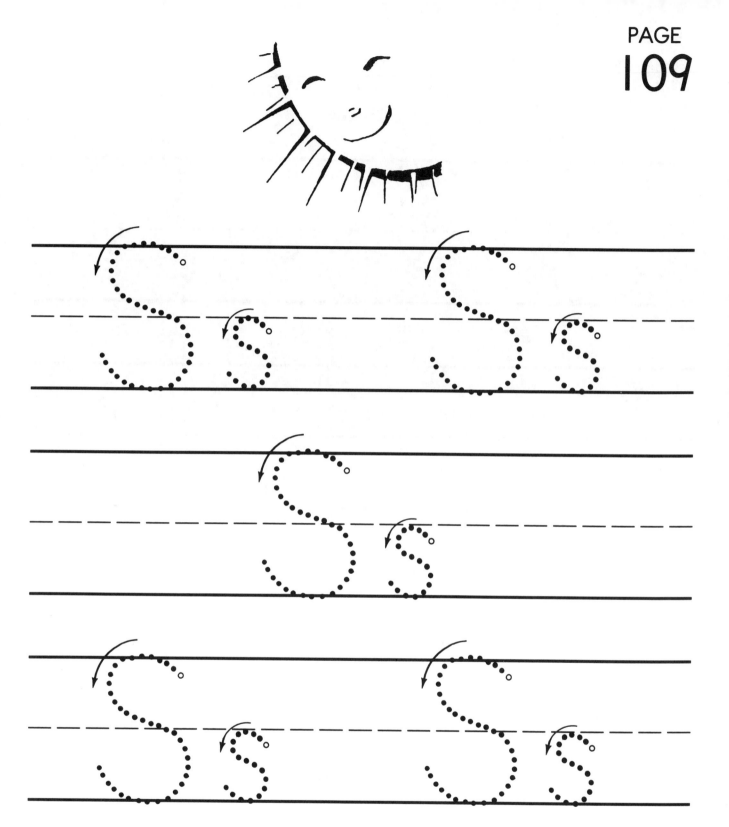

What You Say Guides The Way

To the teacher: As you form each letter on the chalkboard keep repeating:

(For **S**) "Put your pencil on the start dot. Form letter c up in the top space, then curve around and back. That's big letter **S**! (Say name of letter.) S, s, sun! (Say letter sound as in Phonics Song.)"

(For **s**) "Put your pencil on the start dot. Form a very little c in the top of the space, then curve around and back. Little letter **s**! S, s, sun!"

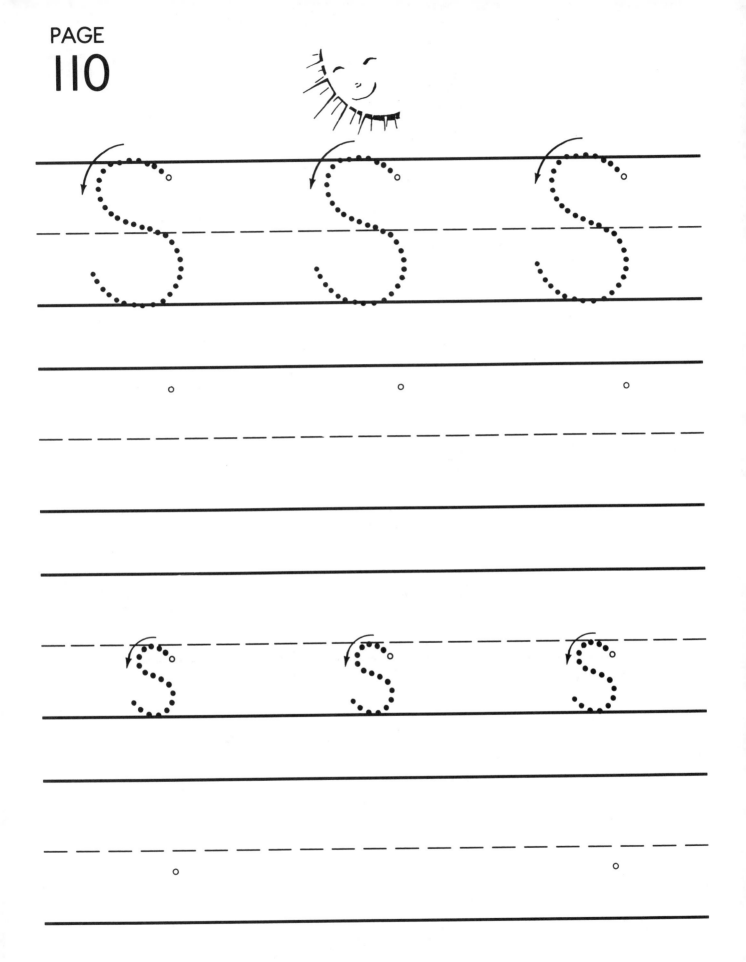

Color, Cut, and Paste
Pictures for S s

To the Teacher: Have students remove this page from book.
Identify items in pictures (seal, bug, wing, leg, snowman, stars, spoon, and a paintbrush).
Have the students cut along dotted lines and paste the pictures that start with the letter **S** sound on the next page.

Name

My Pictures for

S 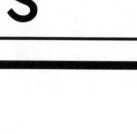 s

Directions: Have students remove page from book. Then have them paste the pictures that start with the correct letter sound into the frames.

My Magazine Picture for

S s

Directions: Have student cut a picture from a magazine and paste in the frame.

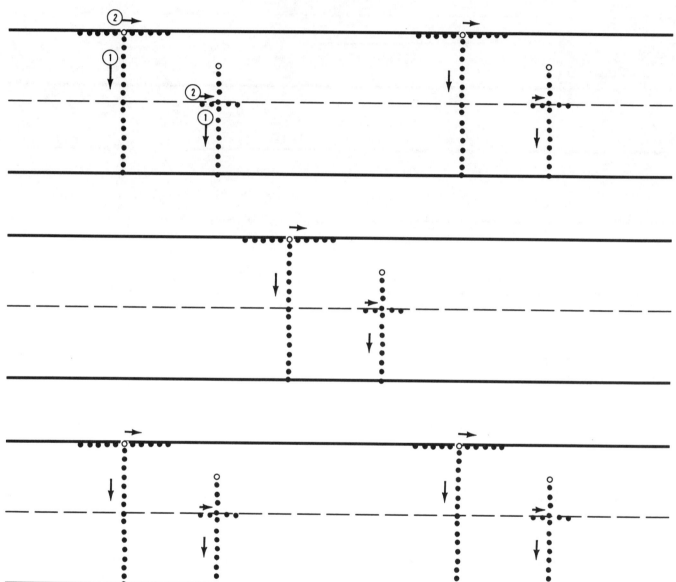

What You Say Guides The Way

To the teacher: As you form each letter on the chalkboard keep repeating:

(For **T**) "Put your pencil on the start dot. Go down straight to the floor and then put his hat on. That's big letter **T**! (Say name of letter.) T, t, tail! (Say letter sound as in Phonics Song.)"

(For **t**) "Put your pencil on the start dot. Little **t** is a teenager. He's not as tall as the Capital letters nor as short as the small letters. Go down to the floor and then go across on the broken line. Little letter **t**! T, t, tail!"

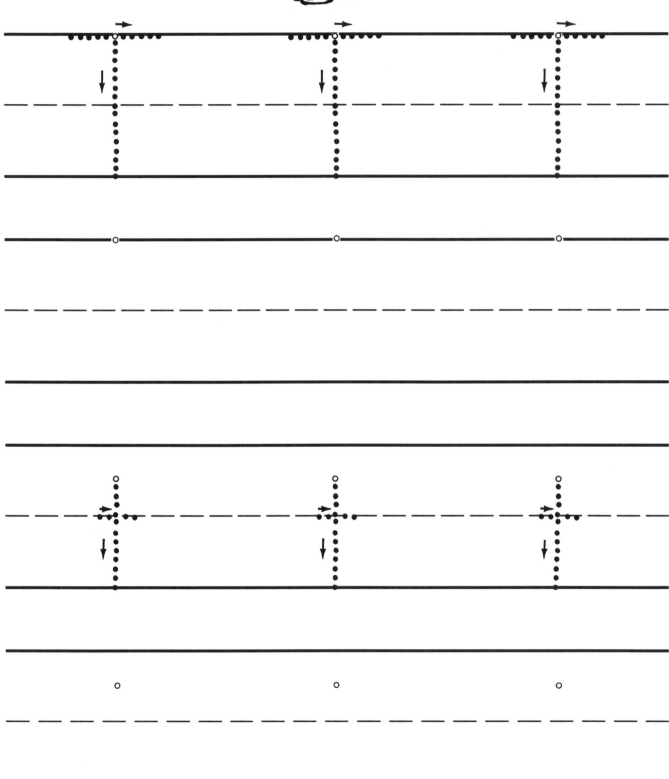

Color, Cut, and Paste
Pictures for T🐿t

To the Teacher: Have students remove this page from book.
Identify items in pictures (book, tire, sun, number "2", toes, camel elbow, and the number "10").
Have the students cut along dotted lines and paste the pictures that start with the letter **T** sound on the next page.

Name

My Pictures for

T  †

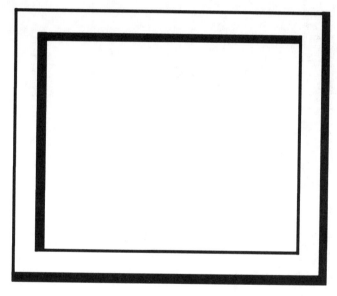

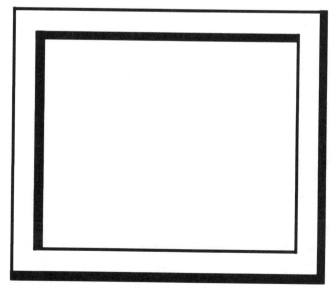

Directions: Have students remove page from book. Then have them paste the pictures that start with the correct letter sound into the frames.

My Magazine Picture for

T   t

Directions: Have student cut a picture from a magazine and paste in the frame.

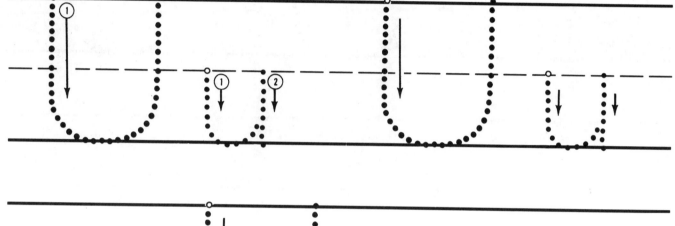

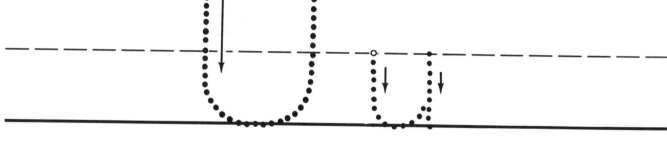

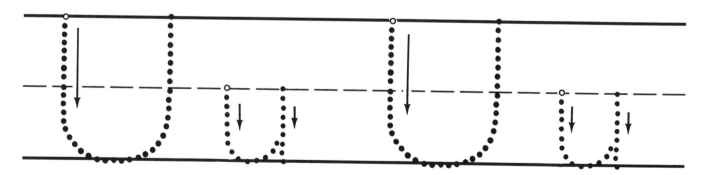

What You Say Guides The Way

To the teacher: As you form each letter on the chalkboard keep repeating:

(For **U**) "Put your pencil on the start dot. Go down to the floor and curve over and up to the top. That's big letter **U**! (Say name of letter.) Ŭ, ŭ, umbrella! (Say letter sound as in Phonics Song.)

(For **u**) "Put your pencil on the start dot. Go down to the floor and curve over and up to the broken line, then straight down to the floor again. Little letter **u**! U, u, umbrella."

Color, Cut, and Paste
Pictures for **U** ☂ **u**

Name

My Pictures for

U u

Directions: Have students remove page from book. Then have them paste the pictures that start with the correct letter sound into the frames.

© 1993 Sue Dickson, International Learning Systems   It is an infringement of Copyright Law to reproduce these pages. Please **DO NOT COPY**

My Magazine Picture for

U u

Directions: Have student cut a picture from a magazine and paste in the frame.

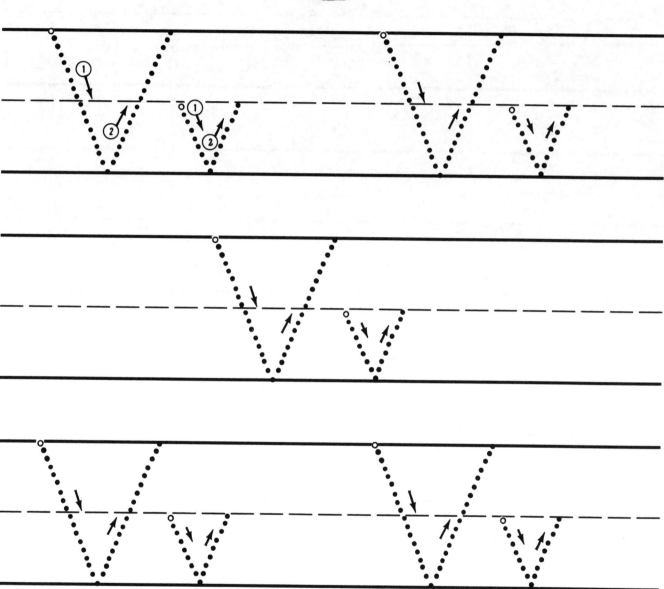

What You Say Guides The Way

To the teacher: As you form each letter on the chalkboard keep repeating:

(For **V**) "Put your pencil on the start dot. Go down the slide to the floor, and up the slide to the ceiling. That's big letter **V**! (Say name of letter.) V, v, vase! (Say letter sound as in Phonics Song.)"

(For **v**) "Put your pencil on the start dot. Go down the slide to the floor, and up the slide to the middle broken line. Little letter **v**! V, v, vase!"

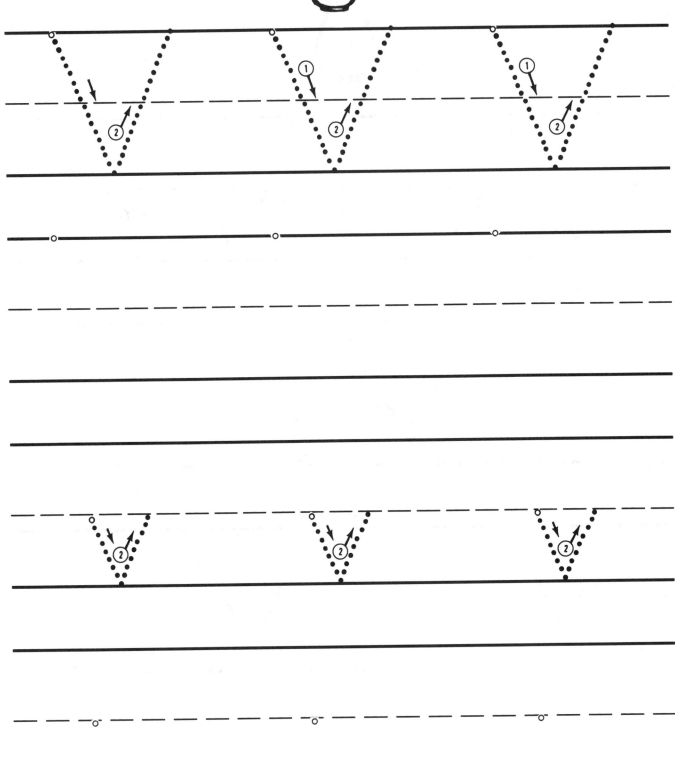

Color, Cut, and Paste
Pictures for V v

To the Teacher: Have students remove this page from book.

Identify items in pictures (vase, goose, jar, van, top, vest, vine, and a man).

Have the students cut along dotted lines and paste the pictures that start with the letter **V** sound on the next page.

Name

My Pictures for

V V

Directions: Have students remove page from book. Then have them paste the pictures that start with the correct letter sound into the frames.

© 1993 Sue Dickson, International Learning Systems   It is an infringement of Copyright Law to reproduce these pages. Please **DO NOT COPY**

My Magazine Picture for

V  v

Directions: Have student cut a picture from a magazine and paste in the frame.

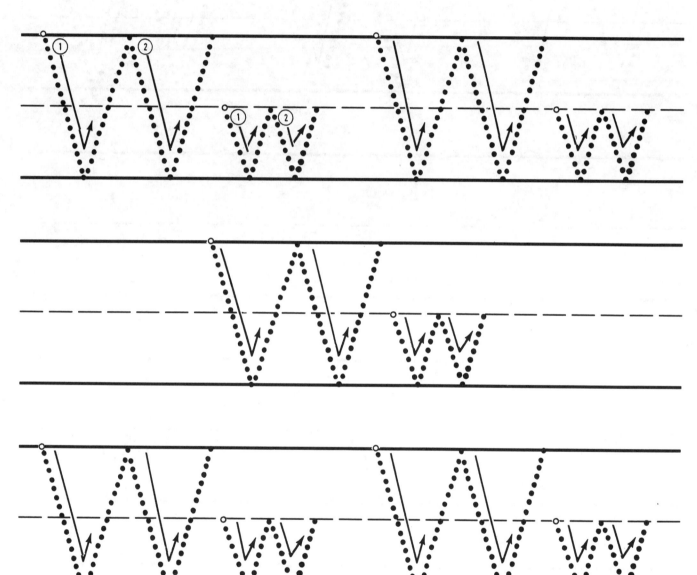

What You Say Guides The Way

To the teacher: As you form each letter on the chalkboard keep repeating:

(For **W**) "Put your pencil on the start dot. Go down the slide to the floor, then up the slide to the ceiling. Then go down the slide and up again to the ceiling. That's big letter **W**! (Say name of letter.) W, w, wagon! (Say letter sound as in Phonics Song.)"

(For **w**) "Put your pencil on the start dot. Go down the slide to the floor, then up the slide to the middle broken line. Then go down the slide and up again to the middle broken line. Little letter **w**! W, w, wagon!"

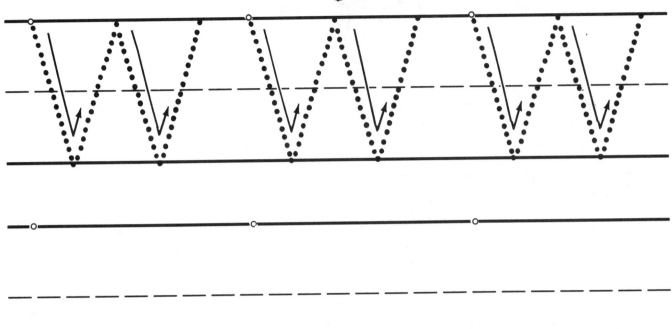

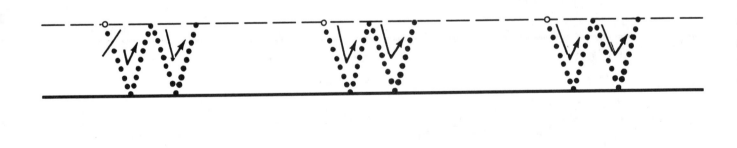

Color, Cut, and Paste
Pictures for W 🛒 w

Name

My Pictures for

W W

Directions: Have students remove page from book. Then have them paste the pictures that start with the correct letter sound into the frames.

My Magazine Picture for

W   W

Directions: Have student cut a picture from a magazine and paste in the frame.

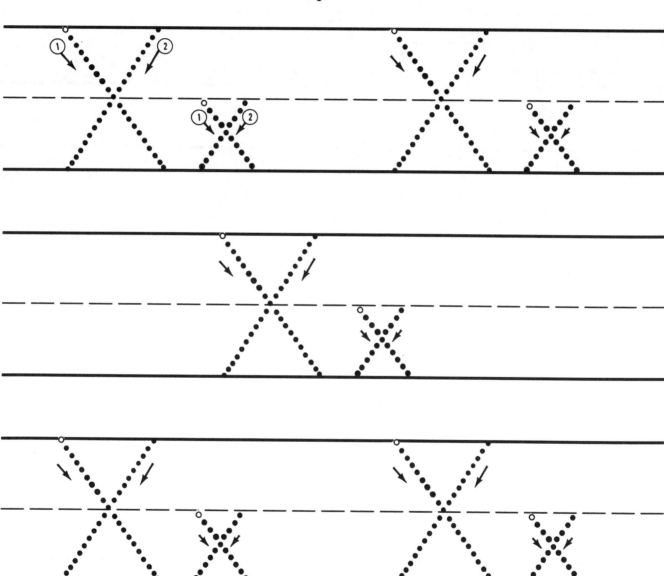

What You Say Guides The Way

To the teacher: As you form each letter on the chalkboard keep repeating:

(For **X**) "Put your pencil on the start dot. Go down the slide to the floor. Now put your pencil up on the ceiling line again and go back down and cross the slide at the broken line and continue to the floor. That's big letter **X**! (Say name of letter.) X, x, (cks!), box! (Say letter sound as in Phonics Song.)"

(For **x**) "Put your pencil on the start dot. Go down the slide to the floor. Now put your pencil up on the middle broken line again and go back down and cross the slide in the middle and continue to the floor. Little letter **x**! X, x, (cks!), box!"

PAGE
140

Color, Cut, and Paste
Pictures for Xx

To the Teacher: Have students remove this page from book.
Identify items in pictures (picture, fox, queen, ax, six, sled, wax, and a turkey).
Have the students cut along dotted lines and paste the pictures that start with the letter **X** sound on the next page.

My Pictures for

X x

Directions: Have students remove page from book. Then have them paste the pictures that start with the correct letter sound into the frames.

© 1993 Sue Dickson, International Learning Systems   It is an infringement of Copyright Law to reproduce these pages. Please **DO NOT COPY**

My Magazine Picture for

X   x

Directions: Have student cut a picture from a magazine and paste in the frame.

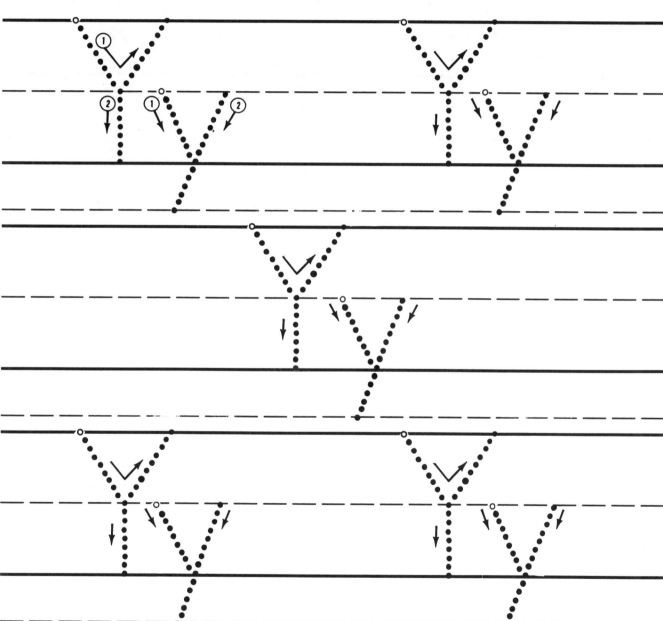

What You Say Guides The Way

To the teacher: As you form each letter on the chalkboard keep repeating:

(For **Y**) "Put your pencil on the start dot. Go down the slide to the center, up the slide to the top, and then put on the stem. That's big letter **Y**! (Say name of letter.) Y, y, yard! (Say letter sound as in Phonics Song.)"

(For **y**) "Put your pencil on the start dot. Go down the slide to the floor line. Put your pencil on the middle broken line again and over a bit, then go down to touch the slide and keep going through to the basement. Little letter **y**! Y, y, yard!"

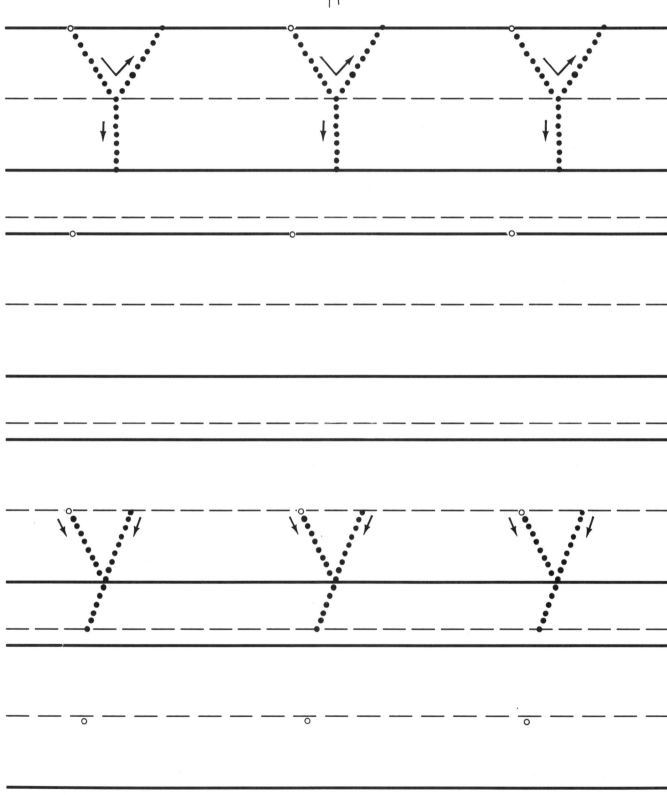

Color, Cut, and Paste
Pictures for Y y

To the Teacher: Have students remove this page from book.
Identify items in pictures (yard stick, cheese, yarn, hanger, butterfly, yell, comb, and a yo-yo).
Have the students cut along dotted lines and paste the pictures that start with the letter **Y** sound on the next page.

Name

My Pictures for

Y 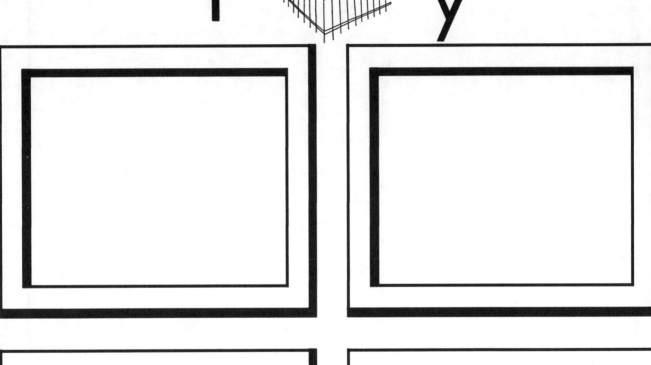 y

My Magazine Picture for

Y y

Directions: Have student cut a picture from a magazine and paste in the frame.

It is an infringement of Copyright Law to reproduce these pages. Please **DO NOT COPY.**

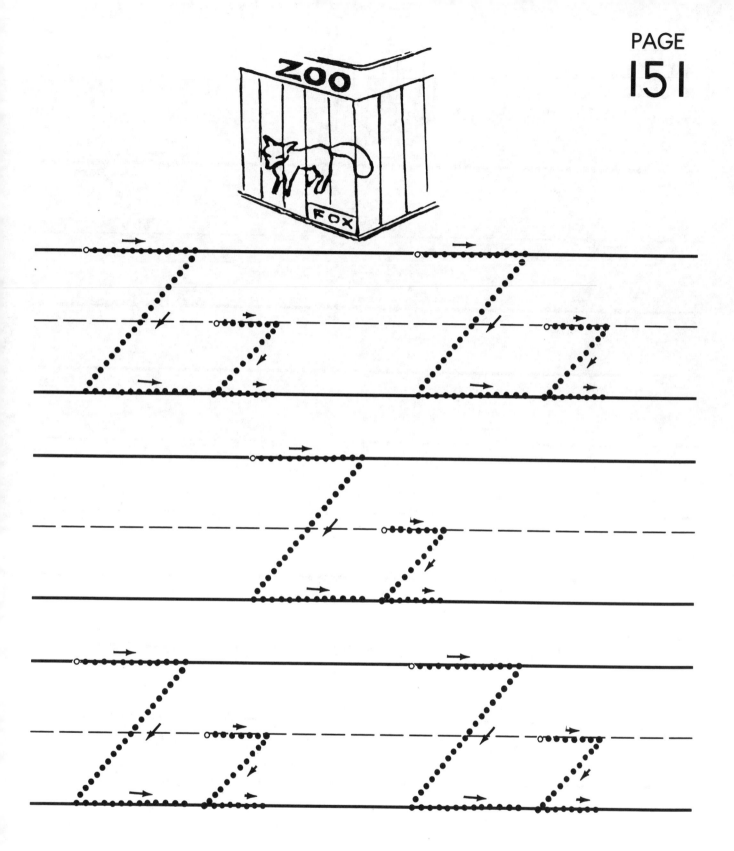

What You Say Guides The Way

To the teacher: As you form each letter on the chalkboard keep repeating:

(For **Z**) "Put your pencil on the start dot. Go across the ceiling, down the slide to the floor (like #7), and back across the floor. That's big letter **Z**! (Say name of letter.) Z, z, zoo! (Say letter sound as in Phonics Song.)"

(For **z**) "Put your pencil on the start dot. Go across the middle broken line, down the slide to the floor, and back across the floor. Little letter **z**! Z, z, zoo!"

ZOO

FOX

Color, Cut, and Paste
Pictures for Z z

To the Teacher: Have students remove this page from book.
Identify items in pictures (cup, zoo, zero, envelope, guitar, zebra, socks, and a zipper).
Have the students cut along dotted lines and paste the pictures that start with the letter **Z** sound on the next page.

Name

_ _

My Pictures for

Z  z

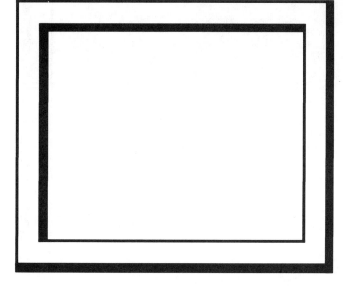

Directions: Have students remove page from book. Then have them paste the pictures that start with the correct letter sound into the frames.

My Magazine Picture for

Z

z

Directions: Have student cut a picture from a magazine and paste in the frame.